NOTRE-DAME DE PARIS

Youth Guide

1163: NOTRE DAME

1248:
SAINTE-CHAPELLE

13TH CENTURY: LOUVRE

1670:
DÔME DES INVALIDE
(HEIGHT: 105M)

A VERY OLD BUILDING

**Notre Dame is very old,
more than eight centuries.**

Work began in 1163 and was finished a hundred years later.
However, the builders were thinking about all the people
who would come here throughout the centuries.

1857:
GARNIER OPERA HOUSE

1889:
EIFFEL TOWER
(HEIGHT: 307M)

1969:
MOUNT PARNASSUS
TOWER
(HEIGHT: 220M)

1977:
POMPIDOU
CENTER

The cathedral can seat as many people as ten metro trains together! Every day people come and adore the Lord, telling him their sufferings and joys and asking his help. Many tourists from all over the world also come to admire the cathedral.

TEXT: MARIE-JEANNE COLONI
ENGLISH TRANSLATION: MARYELLEN O'KEEFE, OSU
ENGLISH EDITOR: MARY-CABRINI DURKIN
ILLUSTRATIONS: HERVÉ VITAL

LAYOUT: MR CHARLY
GRAPHIC DOCUMENTATION: MADELINE DIENNER
ENGRAVING: EDS - 106311
ISBN: 2-7468-1454-4
PRINTED IN CHINA BY SUN FUNG OFFSET BINDING COMPANY LIMITED

TABLE OF CONTENTS

AN ARCHITECTURAL MASTERPIECE

Notre Dame of Paris is located on the Ile de la Cité, birthplace of Paris, and bordered by the Seine River. It is a masterpiece of Gothic art, with remarkable harmony. The church testifies to the faith of those who built it. It contains works of art hidden from the eyes of people, done only for God. Only the most beautiful, the most grand, is suitable to give God glory. This Catholic church is a cathedral. Here the Archbishop of Paris has his official chair, which we call a cathedra.

A POETIC MARVEL

Notre Dame of Paris was constructed so that people might come to meet God in a large crowd or in personal prayer. It invites people to peace and prayer.

In the central portal is found the ring of the right to asylum: Formerly, those who seized it escaped the assailants who were chasing them, because this cathedral is an asylum (a safe place) for all.

On the hinges of the portals decorated with leaves and fruits, beautiful birds are sculpted, singing at the reopening of the Garden of Eden. Let us go there…

To teach about the joy of being in God's presence, Bishop Maurice de Sully used to tell stories. To illustrate the joy of entering into Paradise, where time does not matter, some birds, flowers, and fruits were fashioned on the hinges that held the planks of the doors: they symbolize the Garden of Paradise, the garden of delights where God had placed Adam and Eve. To a person who expressed the desire to know what Paradise was like, the Bishop said that God sent an angel in the form of a bird…. The person was interested enough to stay three hundred years to hear it sing. "Imagine Paradise," cried Maurice, "if the single song of an angel could put someone into such an ecstasy as to mistake three hundred years for an hour!"

(M. M. Martin "A Great Bishop of the West")

A HISTORY BOOK

A symbol of Paris, this cathedral has always witnessed important political and religious events.

The historian Michelet said the same thing: "Notre Dame is itself a history book."

We cannot list all the deeds that have unfolded, but let's recall the following: Notre Dame was not yet completed when the Parisians paid their respects to the body of the deceased St. Louis. Here Philip the Handsome opened the first Estates General (legislative body) of the kingdom of France (1302). King Henry IV married Marguerite de Valois here (1572), then converted solemnly to Catholicism (1594). Pope Pius VII crowned Napoleon first Emperor of the French (1804). At Notre Dame the **Te Deum** was sung for the victory in World War II (1945), and Pope John Paul II proclaimed the beatification of Frederic Ozanam in 1997 during the World Youth Congress. Recalling more recent events: In 2005, the faithful came to Mass to welcome Monsignor Vingt-trois, the successor of the Archbishop of Paris, Cardinal Lustiger. At Notre Dame the faithful also gathered to thank God for Pope John Paul II and await the naming of the new head of the Church, Pope Benedict XVI.

NOTRE DAME IS CONSECRATED TO THE VIRGIN MARY

Notre Dame of Paris seeks particularly to honor the Virgin Mary; it is consecrated to her. It contains thirty-seven pictures of the Virgin.

Eudes de Sully, successor to Maurice de Sully,
the first builder-bishop,
gave an ending to the "Hail Mary,"
the prayer drawn from Luke's gospel (Lk 1:39),
by adding, "Pray for us sinners now and
at the hour of our death."

"Hail Mary, full of grace.
The Lord is with you. Blessed
are you among women and
blessed is the fruit of your womb,
Jesus. Holy Mary, mother of God,
pray for us sinners, now and at
the hour of our death. Amen."

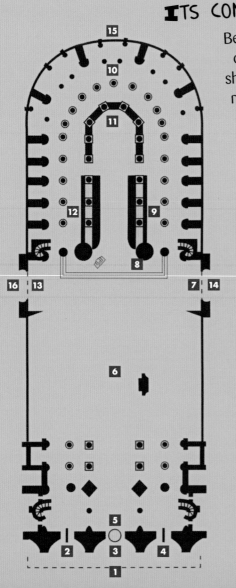

ITS CONSTRUCTION IS A SPIRITUAL MESSAGE

Because the Christian faith recognizes in Jesus the Light of the World, Notre Dame of Paris appears like a great ship facing toward the east, the direction where the sun rises. It is built in the form of a cross to recall the cross of Christ, who saves all and gathers all.

Notre Dame measures 130 meters long, 48 meters wide, 35 meters high, and can hold 5000 people.

1 West façade
2 Portal of the Coronation of the Virgin
3 Portal of the Last Judgment
4 Portal of St. Anne
5 West rose window
6 Nave
7 South rose window
8 Virgin of the Pillar: Notre Dame de Paris
9 South wall of the choir: the Resurrection
10 Apse
11 Choir
12 North wall of the choir: Christmas and the Passion
13 North rose window
14 Portal of St. Stephen
15 Chevet
16 Portal of Cloister Street

During important events like the coming of the Pope or the ordination of priests every June, Notre Dame seems too small. Many people have to assist at the ceremony from outside in the square. Then they can admire the great façade of the cathedral.

Sculptures and stained glass recall the history of the people of God, the life of Jesus and the lives of Christians.

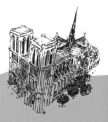

The first, the one who decided to build this cathedral, was Bishop Maurice. He was born about 1120 at Sully on the Loire. (That is why he is called Maurice de Sully.) They say that his mother was a woodcutter who brought logs from the woods to the Abbey of St. Benedict on the Loire. Maurice went to school there.

Named Bishop of Paris in 1160, Maurice decided to give the capital city a cathedral worthy of the principal city in France.

King Louis VII, his classmate, favored the project. The Church, the prominent people of the city, and all the people participated. Some offered money, others their labor or their expertise.

Construction began in 1163. The first stone was set in place by Pope Alexander III and King Louis VII. Maurice de Sully oversaw the building site for 33 years, but Notre Dame was not completed until 1272, under St. Louis, King Louis IX.

For a century, all the groups of artisans worked continuously under the direction of experienced architects.

No one can forget all these builders.
Maurice de Sully and King Louis VII are carved on the portal to the right of the façade, called the portal of St. Anne; on the door of the Cloister side, one can admire St. Louis and his wife, Marguerite of Provence. The name of one of the architects, Jean de Chelles, is sculpted on the south wall of the cathedral

Finally, thousands of men and women have worked on this cathedral. One and all offered their efforts to God and Mary.

AN IMMENSE BUILDING SITE

To begin construction, Bishop Maurice de Sully opened a new road to transport the necessary materials: the beams for the framework. In total, nearly twenty-one hectares (about 50 acres) of oak trees were needed for the framework of Notre Dame. This is why they call it "the forest." But also 1320 sheets of lead for roofing that weighs more than 210 tons, 420,000 pounds.

The stone came from the quarries of Bièvre and was shipped on boats along the Seine River and unloaded on the dock of the Ile de la Cité.

On the building site, operations began.
Unskilled laborers,
apprentices, hundreds
of specialized workers,
and volunteers—all were
guided by the
masters who directed
construction:
the mason,
the carpenter,
the glass artist.

Do not think that only
men worked on this immense edifice!
A great number of women
according to their strength and their talents
participated in the construction
of Notre Dame in Paris.
Some worked with mortar,
some with plaster,
others in decorating.

A NEW STYLE OF ARCHITECTURE

Notre Dame in Paris is a Gothic cathedral. This was the new architectural style that originated at that time because of technical developments. The builders could place all the weight of the structure on the pillars rather than on the walls. Therefore, the interior had maximum space and light.

Abbot Suger, friend of Maurice de Sully, had already built the first French ribbed arches in the Basilica of St. Denis. This new form of architecture, called Gothic, allows better balancing of weight, particularly as a result of the crossed ribbed arches and the exterior flying buttresses which absorb the pressure from the walls, directing it into the ground. Therefore it is possible to cut large, high windows into the walls.

The middle of the cathedral is called the nave. It resembles the path of a garden and is bordered by columns crowned with foliage.
With the nave, the arms of the transept form a cross.

Light comes from three large, stained-glass rose windows and beautifully lights up the interior of the cathedral, changing hour by hour.

Chapels dedicated to different groups extend all around the building.

The rose windows, like roses with multicolored glass petals, represent the flowers of Paradise. Each colored petal adds to the beauty of the others, and the result is not only for the sake of beauty, but also has a spiritual meaning. Each person is unique, but the children of God are still more beautiful when united!

To see the completion of the three large thirteen-meter rose windows, St. Louis the King delayed for several months his departure for the Second Crusade. That was in 1270, and he never returned.

A PLACE OF INVENTIONS

This building project was unusual.
How could they raise the walls so high?
How could they position the roof?
How could they find all the necessary workers?

As fast as problems presented themselves, the workers found solutions.
So, the stones were carried on the backs of men in baskets or on stretchers.

When the wheelbarrow was invented at a similar site, it gave noble service; a single person could do the work of two people!

At the same time, to lift the building materials one by one, the craftsmen used cranes, winches, and also a sort of wheeled vehicle called a "squirrel," activated by walking; they then hoisted a wooden frame that gave the structure strong support.

In this way the workers were able to raise the vaulted ceiling of the cathedral to 33 meters high, the towers to 69 meters and the spire to 90 meters!

In the south tower is a bell called a bourdon (bumblebee). It weighs 13 tons and its clapper a little over 1,000 pounds.

The bourdon rings on Christmas,
Palm Sunday, Easter, the Ascension,
Pentecost, the Assumption,
All Saints and on important occasions.

EXCITEMENT AND WONDER

In the Middle Ages all the prayers were in Latin, a language that the majority of people did not understand. To be better understood, the texts for the big feasts were acted out. Inside the cathedral, sculpted and painted panels hanging on the walls surrounding the choir told the Gospel story.

The celebrations could be called "plays." They began with a presentation of all the actors in costume, with their scripts written on papers that they held in their hands. The characters were dressed as though the events were going on in their own times (the Middle Ages).

These "liturgical plays" used to last so long that it became necessary to separate them from the religious services.

That was when "Mystery Plays" developed on the cathedral square. The façade served as a backdrop for these religious spectacles. The porch represented Paradise.

Several hundred amateur actors would wear the same costumes as the statues decorating the façade: the Kings of Judah, Mary, the prophets.

They also staged the **Miracle of Theophilus** by the storyteller Rutebeuf (about 1260) that we will speak of later on.

The statues were in colors that stood out against a gold background. The sculptures on the portals told stories of the Bible and of the early Christians. So people who could not read could learn and understand biblical history and the lives of the saints.

On this façade, 28 statues of the kings of Judah and of Israel, ancestors of Christ, are represented. Above these figures, on both sides of the façade, are the statues of Adam and Eve. In the center, a large rose window measuring nearly 10 meters forms a halo for the statue of the Virgin Mary who is framed by two angels and presents to us her child, Jesus, the Son of God.

THE PORTALS (DOORWAYS)

THE PORTAL OF THE VIRGIN

On the left of the façade we recognize the prophets who announced her glorious destiny, the kings from whom she descended. Above, the Virgin Mary is represented in eternal rest; as she fell asleep in death, in the presence of Christ and his apostles, she was raised up to heaven. The Church celebrates her being taken up to heaven on August 15, the Feast of the Assumption. Farther above, an angel crowns Mary while Christ, seated on the same throne as his mother, hands her a scepter: Mary is Queen of Heaven.

You can also see St. Denis,
who brought Christianity to the Gauls.
He was the first bishop of Paris
and was decapitated about 250.
To commemorate this martyr,
St. Denis is represented carrying his head
in his hands, as though death
could not touch him.

Opposite him, the patron of Paris, St. Genevieve, holds a candle that a little devil is trying to extinguish. In 451, by her prayers and encouragement— "Children of God, do not fear"—Genevieve protected Paris from the armies of the Huns and their king Attila, known as "the Scourge of God."

The foliage, flowers, and fruits are reminders of heaven, along with angels, patriarchs, kings and prophets. This portal expresses the faith and hope of Christians.

THE PORTAL OF THE LAST JUDGMENT

In the middle of the façade is The Portal of the Last Judgment. Jesus is represented as the one who welcomes us while Mary and St. John pray for humanity. Below is a representation of the Resurrection of the Dead, while in the middle is the Judgment: the chosen are led to heaven by angels; the others, who chose not to love God and their neighbors, are led to hell by demons.

"THEN THE KING WILL SAY TO THOSE ON HIS RIGHT, 'I WAS HUNGRY AND YOU FED ME; THIRSTY AND YOU GAVE ME A DRINK, A STRANGER AND YOU WELCOMED ME, NAKED AND YOU CLOTHED ME, SICK AND YOU VISITED ME, A PRISONER AND YOU CAME TO SEE ME.' THEN THE JUST WILL ASK HIM: 'LORD, WHEN DID WE SEE YOU HUNGRY AND FEED YOU, THIRSTY AND GIVE YOU A DRINK, A STRANGER AND GIVE YOU WELCOME, NAKED AND CLOTHE YOU, SICK OR IMPRISONED AND VISIT YOU?' AND THE KING WILL ANSWER THEM, 'IN THE MEASURE THAT YOU HAVE DONE THIS TO THE LEAST OF MY BROTHERS AND SISTERS, YOU HAVE DONE IT TO ME'"

(MT 25).

THE PORTAL OF ST. ANNE

On the right of the façade is the Portal of St. Anne
honoring the mother of Mary.
The Virgin Mary presents the infant Jesus.
She is surrounded by angels carrying censers.
Bishop Maurice de Sully is represented standing
to the left, King Louis VII is kneeling at the right.
These are the two who wanted to consecrate
the cathedral to the mother of God. Sculptures depict
episodes in Mary's life—the Annunciation, the Visitation,
the Nativity, the adoration of the Magi. The grandparents
of Jesus, St. Anne and St. Joachim, can also be seen.

THE PORTAL OF ST. STEPHEN

St. Louis planned this portal to the south
facing the Latin Quarter in homage to
St. Stephen, who was killed by stoning
for preaching the Gospel.

Some scenes depict the life of students
and professors of the University of Paris
founded by the Church. Poor students
were fed for free with money collected
on the Feast of the Epiphany.

THE PORTAL OF CLOISTER STREET

This portal was built to the north around 1250 by John de Chelles. Its large rose window measures 13 meters in diameter. The sculptures show the role of Mary in the childhood of Jesus.

Here the artist wanted to depict the lowliness of the crib, the Presentation in the Temple in Jerusalem, the persecution by King Herod, and the Flight into Egypt.

The legend of St. Theophilus that was enacted on the square is sculpted here. Theophilus, a deacon, had sold his soul to the devil in order to take the place of his bishop. But Theophilus regretted his bargain with Satan and wanted to ask pardon. He asked the Virgin Mary to help him recover peace with God. Mary presented to him the cross of Christ, which conquered the devil. Theophilus regained his freedom. He asked pardon of his bishop, and everyone was happy.

This legend hints at the sacrament of Reconciliation and of Penance.

THE CHILDREN'S CHOIR, THE CHOIR SCHOOL OF NOTRE DAME

In the cloister, the residence of the canons (priests of the cathedral), live some children who are housed and fed and educated for free. In exchange, they are asked to sing in the cathedral for Masses and other religious ceremonies. Thus, at midnight on December 24, two children of the Choir School announce Christmas by singing,

"A child is born for us in Bethlehem, alleluia."

An artist has depicted them on the wall of the choir as Christmas angels announcing the birth of the Savior.

THE LIFE OF JESUS

To encourage meditation,
a wall shutting out noise surrounds the choir,
forming a chapel within the great cathedral.

On this wall are sculpted scenes from the life of Jesus.
On the north side, you can see **the Visitation, the angels'
announcement to the shepherds, the Nativity**
—where the artist has placed Jesus above Mary
to signify that he is the most important person.

The Adoration of the Magi—Melchior, Gaspar, and Balthazar—before Jesus, held by the Virgin Mary. They offer Jesus their presents, gold, incense, and myrrh. The one in front of Jesus has placed his crown on the ground.

In the Middle Ages, on the day of Epiphany, children sold round loaves of bread to pilgrims, singing, **"You cannot go to Bethlehem, but if you help young people, Jesus will receive your gifts."** In the evening, a large procession would bring to the cathedral all the money collected, assuring poor students support for the whole year. What was once the bread of pilgrims has become king-cakes.

Now we see **the massacre of the innocents** and **the Flight into Egypt**. In those days, the Law of Moses required that Jewish parents present a son to the Lord forty days after his birth. We see **the Presentation of Jesus in the Temple**; in the background, behind Mary, a woman holds a basket with two turtledoves given in sacrifice. If she seems to look at us, it is to remind us to thank God as the Virgin Mary did in presenting her son in the Temple.

The following scenes show **Jesus among the doctors of the law**, where Jesus is depicted as very young, but leading the discussion; **the baptism of Jesus; the Wedding Feast of Cana** where Mary presents a request that leads to Jesus' first miracle.

When Mary calls the servants and says:
"Do whatever he tells you"
she gives us a lesson.
She speaks also to us!

Here is the representation of Holy Week: **the entrance into Jerusalem**, then **the Last Supper of Jesus** and **the washing of Peter's feet** by Jesus before he celebrates the Paschal feast with his disciples.

The apostle Peter holds the book of Scriptures. The apostles will go from here to the whole world to announce the Good News.

The Supper is the last meal that Jesus shared with his disciples before Easter. "DURING THE MEAL, JESUS TOOK BREAD, THANKED GOD, BROKE IT AND GAVE IT TO HIS DISCIPLES SAYING: 'TAKE AND EAT, ALL OF YOU, FOR THIS IS MY BODY.' THEN HE TOOK THE WINE, AND AFTER HAVING THANKED GOD, HE GAVE IT TO THEM SAYING, 'DRINK OF IT, ALL OF YOU, THIS IS MY BLOOD, THE BLOOD OF THE NEW COVENANT, WHICH WILL BE SHED FOR ALL IN PARDON FOR THEIR SINS' " (MT 26:26).

The first covenant between God and the Jewish people became with Christ a covenant between God and all humanity.

The following scene shows us **Jesus in the Garden of Olives** where he is depicted with his disciples after the Paschal meal. He has gone some distance from his disciples to pray to God: **"My Father, if it is possible, take away from me this cup of suffering. However, not what I want, but whatever you want"** (Mt. 36:39).

In the tradition of the Jewish meal, at the end of the meal as we saw at the Last Supper, the guests pass a cup around and each one drinks from it, one after another, as a sign of union.

In the Middle Ages, to better understand, they used a legend, that of the tree of life. From the beginning, doubting God, humanity in Paradise spoiled the tree of life. However, the seeds of the tree were pushed into the earth, giving birth to different trees instead of just one, and symbolizing rupture and disunion.

Jesus prays alone.
He receives from his Father the book of Scriptures that foretell his Passion and his Resurrection.

Unfortunately, the wall that continues to recount the life of Jesus and his death on the cross has disappeared today.
Along the south side of the choir wall, scenes depict the **appearances of Jesus** after his Resurrection.

And here is the continuation of **the tree of life**.
Behind **Jesus** the trees are now close together precisely because by his death and Resurrection Jesus has reunited humanity. The crown of golden fruits recalls the sacraments.
According to the Gospels, it was Mary Magdalen who met Jesus first, but she did not recognize him right away; she thought that he was the gardener. The artist represents Jesus holding in his hand a spade.

Following are **the appearances to the holy women and to St. Peter**, before **the appearance to the disciples of Emmaus**. On the evening of his Resurrection, Jesus rejoins his discouraged disciples walking along the road. When Jesus catches up with them, they do not recognize him, but they confide their sadness at having seen Jesus crucified. Jesus listens and speaks to them, but the disciples still do not recognize him. However, the disciples feel good in the presence of this man, and invite him to have dinner with them. At table, when Jesus breaks the bread to give to them, they finally recognize him; Jesus had done this action on Holy Thursday, while at Supper.

To tell this episode of the gospel the artist has clothed Jesus in shining garments, but the disciples wear the clothing of the Middle Ages, to signify that Jesus lives from age to age.

The story of Jesus continues with **the appearances in the Upper Room** and **to Thomas, the miraculous catch of fish, the commissioning of Peter for his mission** and **the Ascension of Jesus to Heaven.**

A HOUSE OPEN TO ALL

Notre Dame contains many other treasures that we have not presented. The Cathedral of Paris is open to the whole world: to those who come to pray, to those who come to visit. Music holds a privileged place here. Besides the songs of the Choir School there is the playing of celebrated organists.

The clergy—priests and deacons—are present here every day for prayer and Mass, and to greet those who wish to speak with them or receive the sacraments.

For believers, the greatest of all the treasures is the presence of the invisible Christ.

And since this cathedral is dedicated to the Virgin Mary, why not recite this prayer that invites us to preserve a childlike heart?

Prayer to the Virgin

HOLY MARY, MOTHER OF GOD,
PRESERVE FOR ME A CHILDLIKE HEART
PURE AND TRANSPARENT AS A SPRING.
OBTAIN FOR ME A SIMPLE HEART
THAT HAS NO TASTE OF SORROW,
A GREAT HEART, GIVING ITSELF,
TENDER IN COMPASSION,
A HEART FAITHFUL AND GENEROUS,
THAT DOES NOT FORGET ANY GOOD,
NOR HOLD ONTO ANY GRUDGE OR EVIL.
MAKE MY HEART SWEET AND HUMBLE,
LOVING WITHOUT DEMANDING A RETURN,
REJOICING IN LOSING ITSELF IN ANOTHER HEART,
BEFORE YOUR DIVINE SON.
A HEART LARGE AND INVINCIBLE
THAT NO INGRATITUDE CAN HARDEN
THAT NO INDIFFERENCE CAN WEARY.
A HEART TORMENTED BY THE GLORY OF JESUS CHRIST
WOUNDED BY HIS LOVE
AND WHOSE WOUND CAN BE CURED ONLY IN HEAVEN.

LET'S PLAY!

EQUIPMENT FOR LIFTING:
Winches and ropes raised loads to the top of the building.
Guess whether the bucket is going up or down,
when the workers turn the cogwheels to the left.

39

1

A

2

B

3

C

ON THE WORK SITE...
The wheelbarrow was invented on the cathedral work sites.
In the past all the workers' associations were found on the work site.

Can you help each worker by connecting him with his tools?

Solution to the puzzle:
1 with A
2 with C
3 with B

WINDOWS LIKE ROSES
You can imitate the rose-window-makers at Notre Dame.
On the white spaces paste colored paper that you can cut out of old magazines.
You will notice that the shades are affected when different colors are next to each other.

PORTAL OF ST. ANNE -
SEAT OF WISDOM.
Look carefully at these two images
of the Virgin and find 7 differences
between the two designs.

Solution of the puzzle:
1 Jesus' fingers on the book 2 Designs in Jesus' halo
3 Window of the house, above left 4 Skylight window, above left
5 Part of the throne, bottom left 6 Design left on Jesus' collar 7 Ring on Mary's scepter

BIBLE

The ancient Hebrews collected the sacred writings that God had inspired authors to compose about their religion and combined them into books that we call the Bible. Jesus often quoted passages from the Bible. Christians preserved these texts and added to them the four Gospels, the account of the early Church, letters that apostles had written to the first Christian communities, and the Book of Revelation, the book about God's plans for humanity.

CHOIR

In the church, the space for public prayers offered by the priests and sometimes sung solemnly by a choral group called the choir. At Notre Dame in Paris, it seemed necessary for the choir to be protected by a wall, from the place where the choral group sings, so that the place of prayer remains silent.

CHOIR SCHOOL

In the ninth century, Charlemagne had free elementary schools set up in all the cathedrals and abbeys in his whole empire, to teach reading and writing to all children, even if their parents had no money for their education. The cathedral of Paris did even more; its school led up to university entrance. Students were given room, board and education for free by the cathedral priests, their teachers. In return, the students "paid with their voices" by singing for solemn religious services in the cathedral.

CORPORATIONS

In the Middle Ages, workers joined into labor associations, called "corporations," to protect their rights and to guarantee the quality of their work and the training of young apprentices. Each of these corporations was governed by a council that watched out so that the lure of money would not distract Christians from their religious ideals. In Paris, these groups found a haven in side chapels off the nave. Each year on May 1, the corporations thanked the cathedral for welcoming them at no cost; they held a great festival during which they offered decorations for the cathedral.

KINGS OF JUDAH
The crowned figures on the façade of the cathedral of Paris represent the ancestors of Christ, since he was a descendant of David, of the tribe of Judah. David succeeded Saul, Israel's first king. These figures are called "kings of Judah." This rootedness of Jesus in the history of his people is also manifested in the same way on the façades of some other French cathedrals.

LAW OF MOSES
When Moses had gathered the descendants of the patriarch Abraham, he received from God on Mount Sinai a law that would make them into a single people, committed to observing God's commandments.

LITURGY
When the community of believers worships God publicly, their religious service is called "liturgy." It is connected with the tradition of Christian prayer throughout the centuries. Even when an individual prays alone using the official prayers that belong to the liturgy, that person's prayer is also "liturgical."

MESSIAH
Messiah is a Hebrew title applied to Jesus, who was anointed or consecrated for the mission which had been foretold by the ancient prophets. We also speak of him with another name which comes from Greek and means exactly the same thing: "Christ."

PROPHET
This word comes from Greek and means someone who speaks in the name of another. It applies to people who speak in God's name, declaring the meaning of historic events that fulfill God's plan, that is, the well-being of humanity, or pointing out human failures.

SACRED SCRIPTURE
Both Jews and Christians recognize that the books of the Bible were inspired by God, who permitted the prophets and other writers to understand God's message and to write it down. These books are called "sacred Scripture." Muslims share the same respect for the revealed "Book," since they consider that Mohammed carried out the work of a prophet in giving them the Koran.

REFERENCES TO OTHER BOOKS

Many medieval stories illustrated by sculptures in cathedrals are published in the pocket collection, "Folio" by Gallimard.

Sequence on the west façade: Arnould Gréban: " **Le Mystère de la Passion** "
Story of Anne and Joachim, Portal of St. Anne, Jacopo de Voragine, **"The Golden Legend"**
The Works of the Months, around the Portal of the Virgin, west façade: The Shepherds' Calendar
Virtues and Vices, medallions on the west façade: Fables
Tympanum of the Portal of the Virgin, west façade: Jacopo de Voragine, **"The Golden Legend"**
Portal of Cloister Street: Rutebeuf **"The Miracle of Theophilus"**
Rose windows of the transepts, the Red Door, chapels of the corporations: Joinville: **"Histoire du règne de Saint Louis"**
For the Portal of St. Stephen: New Testament, represented according to the Acts of the Apostles.

1163: NOTRE DAME

1248:
SAINTE-CHAPELLE

13ᵀᴴ CENTURY: LOUVRE

1670:
DÔME DES INVALIDE
(HEIGHT: 105M)

46

1857:
GARNIER OPERA HOUSE

1889:
EIFFEL TOWER
(HEIGHT: 307M)

1969:
MOUNT PARNASSUS
TOWER
(HEIGHT: 220M)

1977:
POMPIDOU
CENTER

47

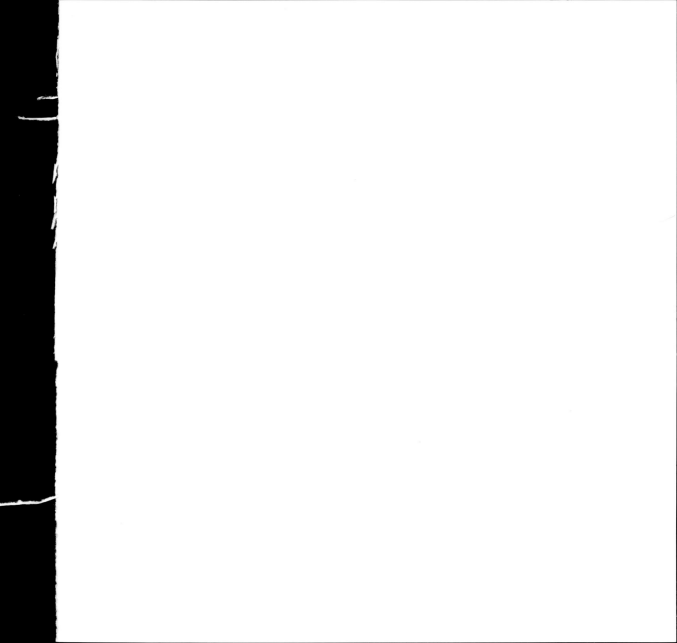